Perfect Pics

Great Pictures for Language Learning

By

Lonnie Dai Zovi

Illustrated by

Ed Saxon

ISBN 13 - 978-0-935301-85-4

Vibrante Press

P.O. Box 51853
Albuquerque. N.M.
87181-1853

Introduction

Perfect Pics© has been developed for all language educators who realize that pictures are indispensable in the language classroom at all levels and all ages. They help in many ways.

- **Visual learners** learn better when they can see what they are learning or hearing.
- Non-readers (either due to age, ability, or unfamiliarity with the writng system) need pictures as they aquire new words.
- **Translation** is not needed if pictures are used and therefore acquisition is faster and more permanent.
- **Activities** and games using pictures are very helpful and fun.
- **Oral work** is made possible with picture stimuli.

Pictures for the language class can be obtained in a variety of ways:

- The teacher or student(s) may draw them.
- The teacher may take photographs.
- They may be cut from magazines and catalogues.
- They may get clip art from the internet (many of which are copyrighted)
- They may purchase clip art books or CDs

All the aforementioned sources are valid and feasible, albeit with problems.

- Many teachers can't draw well and their students are oftern too busy or unwilling to draw the amount of pictures that teachets need.
- Photographs and magazine pictures are lovely but usually there is only one, small and not too easily reproduced.
- Clip art is often really cute but not only does it take an awful lot of time, but seldom are there enough pictures of the theme or subject that you need online or even in most books.

One of the main advantages to using a book such as **Perfect Pics** ©is that there are very many verbs, adjectives and other pictures. These very accessible and ready for you to put on your quizzes, flashcards, games and more. There are pattersn and suggestions for use in the back, as well as keys in many languages.

Also available for purchase is a CD with the pictures (only) for easy placement in documents and more.(www.vibrante.com)

Table of Contents

A 1	**B** 2	**C** 3	**D** 4
E 5	**F** 6	**G** 7	**H** 8
I 9	**J** 10	**K** 11	**L** 12
M 13	**N** 14	**O** 15	**P** 16

A 17	**B** 18	**C** 19	**D** 20
E 30	**F** 40	**G** 50	**H** 60
I 70	**J** 80	**K** 90	**L** 100
M 0	**N** 1/2	**O** 1/3	**P** 1/4

A	B	C	D
E	F	G	H
I	J	K	L
M	N	O	P

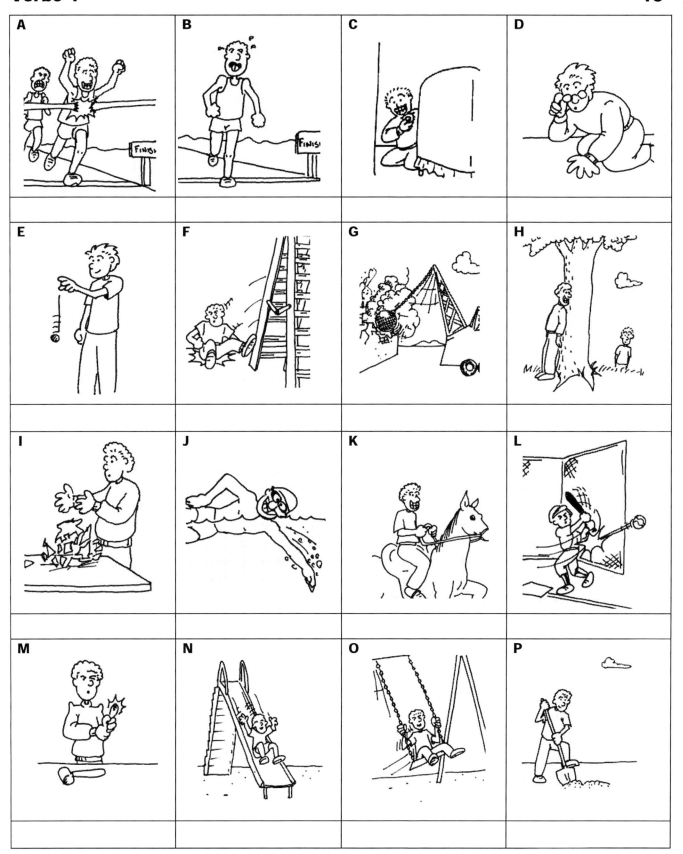

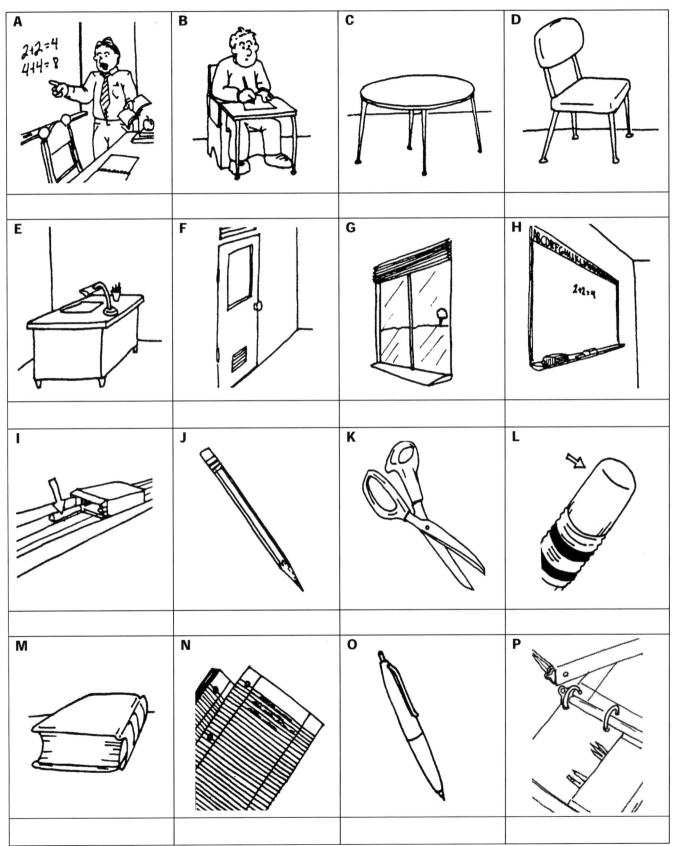

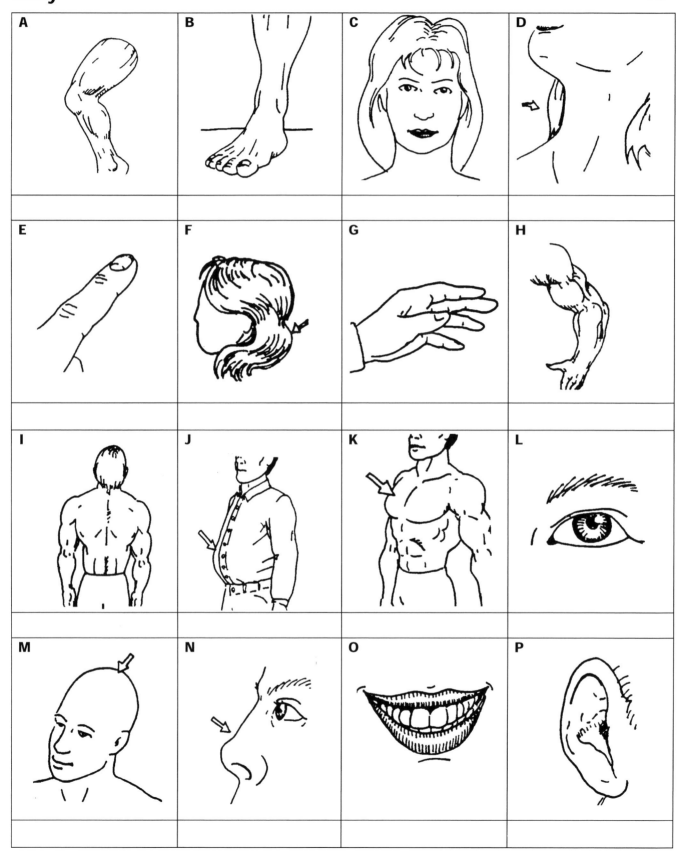

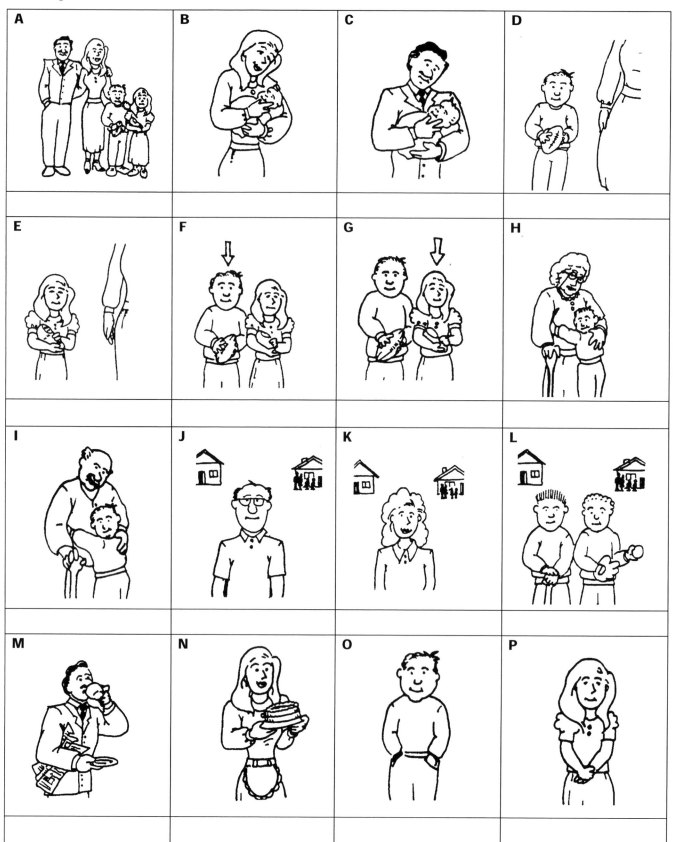

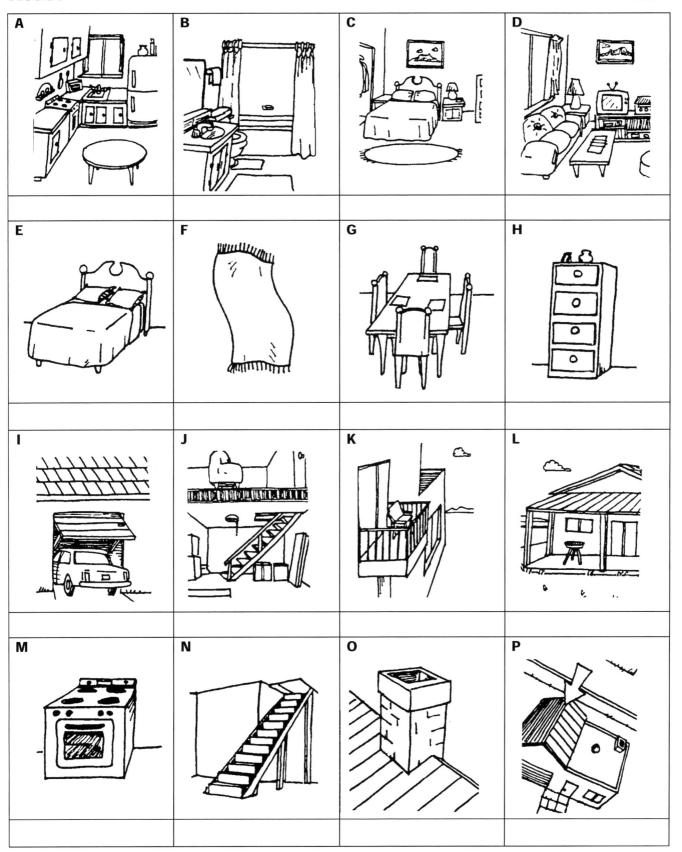

A	B	C	D
E	F	G	H
I	J	K	L
M	N	O	P

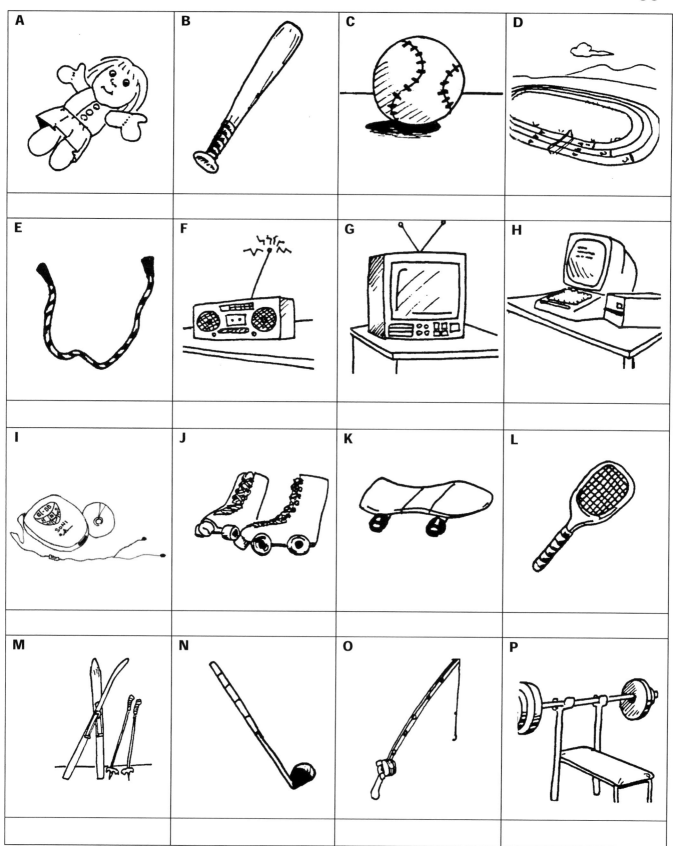

Misc. pronouns for Arabic

A	**B**	**C**	**D**
E	**F**	**G**	**H**
I	**J**	**K**	**L**
M	**N**	**O**	**P**

1. Expressions I

a. Good morning
b. Good afternoon
c. Good evening
d. Bless you
e. What's your name
f. My name is….
g. Hello
h. Good-bye
i. Please
j. Thank you
k. Be careful
l. I like
m. I don't know
n. I know
o. I'm sorry
p. Excuse me

2. Expressions II

a. Let me introduce you,
b. Nice to meet you.
c. What time is it?
d. It's ____ o'clock.
e. What's the date today?
f. It's the 4th of July.
g. How old are you?
h. I'm (6) years old.
i. What's the weather like?
j. How much is this?
k. I don't understand.
l. I'm embarrassed.
m. I'm hungry
n. I'm thirsty.
o. I'm afraid.
p. I'm sleepy.

3. Numbers I

a. one
b. two
c. three
d. four
e. five
f. six
g. seven
h. eight
i. nine
j. ten
k. eleven
l. twelve
m. thirteen
n. fourteen
o. fifteen
p. sixteen

4. Numbers II

a. seventeen
b. eighteen
c. nineteen
d. twenty
e. thirty
f. forty
g. fifty
h. sixty
i. seventy
j. eighty
k. ninety
l. one hundred
m. zero
n. one half
o. one third
p. one fourth

Colors and Misc.

a. red
b. white
c. blue
d. green
e. blue
f. purple
g. orange
h. brown
i. black
j. tired
k. in a hurry
l. in love
m. surprised
n. angry
o. bored
p. funny

6. Pronouns and Symbols

a. I
b. you (fam.)
c. you (form.)
d. he
e. she
f. we (m)
g. we (f)
h. they (m)
i. they (f)
j. you (pl)
k. question
l. negation
m. past tense
n. future tense
o. present tense
p. present progressive

7. Verbs I

a. stand up
b. sit down
c. turn around
d. jump
e. dance
f. sing
g. cry
h. laugh
i. open
j. close
k. kick
l. catch
m. throw
n. play
o. walk
p. run

8. Verbs II

a. read
b. write
c. cut
d. draw
e. paint
f. paste
g. study
h. listen
i. speak, tell
j. take out, carry
k. pick up
l. put away
m. think
n. know
o. ask
p. answer

9. Verbs III

a. eat
b. drink
c. cook
d. wash
e. clean
f. bathe
g. sleep
h. comb hair
i. go to bed
j. get up
k. watch, look at
l. get dressed
m. take off
n. put on
o. brush teeth
p. relax

10. Verbs IV

a. win
b. lose
c. find
d. look for
e. drop
f. fall
g. knock down
h. hide
i. break
j. swim
k. ride
l. hit
m. hurt
n. slide
o. swing
p. dig

11. Verbs V	12. Verbs VI	13. Verbs VII	14. Preposition of Place	15. Adjectives
a. touch	a. sell	a. drive	a. in	a. good
b. see	b. buy	b. crash	b. out (of)	b. bad
c. be born	c. pay	c. go	c. up	c. strong
d. smell	d. want	d. return	d. down	d. weak
e. smile	e. make	e. need	e. in front (of)	e. sick
f. bite	f. carry	f. travel	f. in back (of), behind	f. well
g. scratch	g. give	g. take, carry	g. (to the) right	g. happy
h. pick	h. speak	h. come	h. (to the) left	h. sad
i. grow	i. tear	i. go up	i. around	i. fat
j. crawl	j. work	j. do down	j. on, on top of	j. thin
k. fly	k. fight	k. leave	k. under, beneath	k. tall
l. hear, listen	l. park	l. bring	l. in the middle,	l. short
m. feed	m. fill	m. wait for	between	m. ugly
n. water	n. turn	n. put	m. next to	n. beautiful
o. love	o. follow	o. push	n. through	o. big
p. kiss	p. ride	p. pull	o. near, close	p. small, little
			p. far	

16. Adjectives II	17. Adjectives III	18. School	19. Body	20. Clothes
a. open	a. hot	a. teacher	a. leg	a. dress
b. closed	b. cold	b. student	b. foot	b. skirt
c. clean	c. asleep	c. table	c. face	c. blouse
d. dirty	d. awake	d. chair	d. neck	d. shirt
e. fast	e. tried	e. desk	e. finger	e. pants
f. slow	f. crazy	f. door	f. hair	f. shoes
g. dumb, stupid	g. rotten	g. window	g. hand	g. boots
h. smart, intelligent	h. fresh	h. chalkborad	h. arm	h. socks
i. curly	i. bright, light	i. chalk	i. back	i. jacket, coat
j. straight	j. dark	j. pencil	j. stomach, tummy	j. glove
k. long	k. rich	k. scissors	k. chest	k. hat
l. short	l. poor	l. eraser	l. eye	l. belt
m. close	m. full	m. book	m. head	m. sweater
n. far	n. empty	n. paper	n. nose	n. suit
o. new	o. wet	o. pen	o. mouth	o. tie
p. old	p. dry	p. notebook	p. ear	p. up

21. Family

a. family
b. mother, mom
c. father, dad
d. son
e. daughter
f. brother
g. sister
h. grandmother
i. grandfather
j. uncle
k. aunt
l. cousins
m. man
n. woman
o. boy
p. girl

22. House

a. kitchen
b. bathroom
c. bedroom
d. living room
e. bed
f. rug
g. dining room
h. dresser
i. garage
j. basement
k. balcony
l. patio
m. stove
n. stairs
o. chimmey
p. roof

23. Weather

a. rain
b. It's raining
c. snow
d. it's snowing
e. wind
f. it's windy
g. sun
h. it's sunny
i. clouds
j. it's cloudy
k. it's hot
l. it's cold
m. sky
n. stars
o. moon
p. thermometer

24. Food I

a. rice
b. noodles
c. ham
d. meat
e. fish
f. chicken
g. soup
h. sandwich
i. bread
j. cheese
k. eggs
l. butter
m. cereal
n. sugar
o. salt
p. candy

.Food II

a. cake
b. cookies
c. ice cream
d. juice
e. milk
f. pop, soda
g. ice
h. gum
i. peanut
j. hot dog
k. ham, burger
l. french fries
m. steak
n. jelly, jam
o. peanut butter
p. ketchup

26. Fruit

a. strawberries
b. grapes
c. orange
d. apple
e. cherries
f. lemons
g. watermelons
h. grapefruit
i. pineapples
j. pears
k. banana
l. coconut
m. raspberry
n. raisins
o. tomato
p. fruit

27. Vegetables

a. carrots
b. corn
c. turnip
d. lettuce
e. celery
f. squash
g. broccoli
h. cauliflower
i. peas
j. onion
k. potato
l. pumpkin
m. pickle
n. chili
o. mushroom
p. green beans

28. Nature

a. ocean, sea
b. river
c. lake
d. grass
e. mountains
f. rainbow
g. flower
h. tree
i. rocks
j. mud
k. sand
l. island
m. leaf
n. branch
o. roots
p. weeds

29. Animals I

a. mouse
b. goat
c. rooster
d. pig
e. bird
f. horse
g. hen
h. turkey
i. cat
j. rabbit
k. duck
l. fly
m. fish
n. dog
o. sheep
p. cow

30. Animals II

a. snake
b. turtle
c. bear
d. deer
e. squirrel
f. wolf
g. owl
h. spider
i. porcupine
j. skunk
k. raccoon
l. butterfly
m. ant
n. bee
o. fox
p. frog

31. Animals III

a. zebra
b. camel
c. monkey
d. tiger
e. elephant
f. lion
g. alligator
h. giraffe
i. octopus
j. shark
k. whale
l. bat
m. dinosaur
n. seal
o. kangaroo
p. dolphin

32. Places I

a. forest
b. jungle
c. farm
d. beach
e. bank
f. museum
g. school
h. church
i. desert
j. post office
k. restaurant
l. movies
m. library
n. zoo
o. circus
p. house

33. Places II

a. fire station
b. police station
c. gas station
d. apartments
e. city
f. country
g. swimming pool
h. hospital
i. park
j. factory
k. hotel
l. airport
m. beauty parlor
n. barber shop
o. parking lot
p. store

34. Professions

a. lawyer
b. police
c. carpenter
d. fire fighter
e. pilot
f. waiter
g. doctor
h. nurse
i. mail carrier
j. scientist
k. achitect
l. farmer
m. cashier
n. butcher
o. chef, cook
p. barber

35. Pastimes

a. doll
b. bat
c. ball
d. track
e. jump rope
f. radio
g. television
h. computer
i. CD player
j. roller skates
k. skateboard
l. racket
m. skis
n. golf club
o. fishing rod
p. weights

36. Transportation

a. car, automobile
b. airplane
c. bus
d. train
e. motorcycle
f. bicycle
g. ship
h. boat
i. road
j. train tracks
k. signs
l. headlights
m. flat tire
n. seat
o. seat belt
p. helmet

Keys - Spanish

1. Expresiones I

a. Buenos días
b. Buenas tardes
c. Buenas noches
d. Salud
e. ¿Cómo té llamas ?
f. Me llamo..
g. Hola
h. Adiós
i. Por favor
j. Gracias
k. Ten cuidado
l. Me gusta
m. No sé
n. Yo sé
o. Lo siento
p. Perdón, disculpe

2. Expresiones II

a. Quiero presentarte a...
b. Mucho gusto
c. ¿Qué hora es?
d. Son las…
e. ¿Cuál es la fecha ?
f. Es el….de…..
g. ¿Cuántos años tienes?
h. Tengo….años
i. ¿Qué tiempo hace?
j. ¿Cuánto cuesta?
k. No entiendo
l. Tengo vergüenza
m. Tengo hambre
n. Tengo sed
o. Tengo miedo
p. Tengo sueño

3. Números I

a. uno
b. dos
c. tres
d. cuatro
e. cinco
f. seis
g. siete
h. ocho
i. nueve
j. diez
k. once
l. doce
m. trece
n. catorce
o. quince
p. diez y seis

4. Números II

a. diez y siete
b. diez y ocho
c. diez y nueve
d. veinte
e. treinta
f. cuarenta
g. cincuenta
h. sesenta
i. setenta
j. ochenta
k. noventa
l. cien
m. cero
n. un medio
o. un tercio
p. un cuarto

5. Colores y más

a. rojo
b. blanco
c. amarillo
d. verde
e. azul
f. morado
g. anaranjado
h. café
i. negro
j. cansado
k. de prisa
l. enamorado
m. sorprendido
n. enojado
o. aburrido
p. chistoso

6. Pronombres y más

a. yo
b. tú
c. usted
d. él
e. ella
f. nosotros
g. nosotras
h. ellos
i. ellas
j. ustedes
k. (pregunta)
l. (negación)
m. (pasado)
n. (futuro)
o. (presente)
p. (progresivo)

7. Verbos I

a. pararse
b. sentarse
c. voltearse
d. brincar
e. bailar
f. cantar
g. llorar
h. reírse
i. abrir
j. cerrar
k. patear
l. coger
m. tirar
n. jugar
o. caminar
p. correr

8. Verbos II

a. leer
b. escribir
c. cortar
d. dibujar
e. pintar
f. pegar
g. estudiar
h. escuchar
i. decir, hablar
j. sacar, llevar
k. levantar
l. guardar, alzar
m. pensar
n. saber
o. preguntar
p. contestar

9. Verbos III

a. comer
b. tomar, beber
c. cocinar
d. lavarse
e. limpiar
f. bañarse
g. dormir
h. peinarse
i. acostarse
j. levantarse
k. mirar
l. vestirse
m. quitarse
n. ponerse
o. cepillarse los dientes
p. relajarse, descansar

10. Verbos IV

a. ganar
b. perder
c. encontrar
d. buscar
e. dejar caer
f. caerse
g. tumbar
h. esconder(se)
i. romper
j. nadar
k. montar, pasearse
l. pegar
m. lastimar (se)
n. resbalarse, deslizarse
o. comlumpiarse
p. excavar

11. Verbos V

a. tocar
b. ver
c. nacer
d. oler
e. sonreír
f. morder
g. rasguñar
h. recoger
i. crecer
j. gatearse
k. volar
l. escuchar, oír
m. dar de comer, alimentar
n. regar
o. amar, querer
p. besar

12. Verbos VI

a. vender
b. comprar
c. pagar
d. querer
e. hacer
f. cargar, llevar
g. dar
h. hablar
i. romper
j. trabajar
k. luchar, pelear
l. estacionarse
m. llenar
n. doblar
o. seguir

13. Verbos VII

a. manejar, conducir
b. chocar
c. ir
d. regresar, volver
e. necesitar
f. viajar
g. tomar, agarrar
h. venir
i. subir
j. bajar
k. salir
l. traer
m. esperar
n. poner
o. empujar
p. jalar

14. Preposiciones de lugar

a. en, adentro
b. fuera, afuera
c. arriba
d. abajo, bajo
e. enfrente, delante
f. atrás, detrás
g. (a la) derecha
h. (a la) izquierda
i. alrededor
j. sobre, encima
k. debajo
l. entre, en le medio
m. al lado, junto a
n. por, através
o. cerda
p. lejos

15. Adjetivos

a. bueno
b. malo
c. fuerte
d. débil
e. enfermo
f. bien, sano
g. feliz, alegre
h. triste
i. gordo
j. delardo, flaco
k. alto
l. bajo, chaparro
m. feo
n. bonito, hermoso
o. grande
p. pequeño, chiquito

16. Adjetivos II

a. abierto
b. cerrado
c. limpio
d. sucio
e. rápido
f. despacio
g. tonto
h. inteligente, listo
i. rizado
j. liso
k. largo
l. corto
m. cerca, cercano
n. lejos
o. nuevo
p. viejo

17. Adjetivos III

a. caliente
b. frío
c. dormido
d. despierto
e. cansado
f. loco
g. podrido
h. fresco
i. brillante
j. oscuro
k. rico
l. pobre
m. lleno
n. vacío
o. mojado
p. seco

18. Escuela

a. maestro
b. estudiante
c. mesa
d. silla
e. escritorio
f. puerta
g. ventana
h. pizarra, pizarrón
i. tiza
j. lápiz
k. tijeras
l. borrador
m. libro
n. papel
o. lápiz, boligafo
p. cuaderno

19. Cuerpo

a. pierna
b. pie
c. cara
d. cuello
e. dedo
f. pelo, cabello
g. mano
h. brazo
i. espalda
j. estómago, panza
k. pecho
l. ojo
m. cabeza
n. nariz
o. boca
p. oído, oreja

20. Ropa

a. vestido
b. falda
c. blusa
d. camisa
e. pantalones
f. zapatos
g. botas
h. calcetines
i. chaqueta, abrigo
j. guante
k. sombrero
l. cinturón, faja
m. suéter
n. traje
o. corbata
p. gorra

21. Familia

a. familia
b. madre, mamá
c. padre, papá
d. hijo
e. hija
f. hermano
g. hermana
h. abuela
i. abuelo
j. tío
k. tía
l. primos
m. hombre
n. mujer
o. chico, niño
p. chica, niña

22. Casa

a. cocina
b. baño
c. recámara, cuarto
d. sala
e. cama
f. alfombra
g. comedor
h. buró, tocador
i. garaje
j. sótano
k. balcón
l. patio
m. estufa
n. escalera
o. chimenea
p. techo

23. Tiempo

a. lluvia
b. está lloviendo
c. nieve
d. está nevando
e. viento
f. hace viento
g. sol
h. hace sol
i. nubes
j. está nublado
k. hace calor
l. hace frio
m. cielo
n. estrellas
o. luna
p. termómetro

24. Comida I

a. arroz
b. fideo, tallarín
c. jamón
d. carne
e. pescado
f. pollo
g. sopa
h. sandwich, bocadillo
i. pan
j. queso
k. huevos
l. mantequilla
m. cereal
n. azúcar
o. sal
p. dulces

25. Comida II

a. pastel, torta
b. galletas
c. helado, nieve
d. jugo
e. leche
f. refresco, gaseosa
g. hielo
h. chicle
i. cacahuate, maní
j. hot dog
k. hamburguesa
l. papas fritas
m. bistec, bifstec
n. jalea, mermelada
o. crema de cacahuate
p. catsup

26. Fruta

a. fresas
b. uvas
c. naranja
d. manzana
e. cerezas
f. limón
g. sandía
h. toronja
i. piña
j. pera
k. plátano
l. coco
m. frambuesa
n. datiles
o. tomate
p. fruta

27. Vegetales

a. zanahorias
b. maíz
c. nabo
d. lechuga
e. apio
f. calabacita
g. bróculi
h. coliflor
i. chicharos, guisantes
j. cebolla
k. papa, patata
l. calabaza
m. pepino
n. chile, ají
o. hongo, chamiñon
p. ejotes, judías verdes

28. Naturaleza

a. océano, mar
b. río
c. lago
d. césped, zacate, pasto
e. montañas
f. arco iris
g. flor
h. árbol
i. piedras
j. lodo
k. arena
l. isla
m. hoja
n. rama
o. raíces
p. malas hierbas

29. Animals I

a. ratón
b. chivo
c. gallo
d. puerco, cerdo
e. pájaro
f. caballo
g. gallina
h. pavo, guajolote
i. gato
j. conejo
k. pato
l. mosca
m. pez
n. perro
o. oveja, borrega
p. vaca

30. Animals II

a. víbora, serpiente
b. tortuga
c. oso
d. venado
e. ardilla
f. lobo
g. lechuza, buho
h. araña
i. puerco espín
j. zorrillo
k. mapache
l. mariposa
m. hormiga
n. abeja
o. zorro
p. rana

31. Animals III

a. cebra
b. camello
c. chango, mono, mico
d. tigre
e. elefante
f. león
g. caimán (cocodrilo)
h. jirafa
i. pulpo
j. tiburón
k. ballena
l. murciélago
m. dinosaurio
n. foca
o. canguro
p. delfín

32. Lugares I

a. bosque
b. selva, jungla
c. granja, finca
d. playa
e. banco
f. museo
g. escuela
h. iglesia
i. desierto
j. correo
k. restaturante
l. cine
m. biblioteca
n. zoológico
o. circo
p. casa

33. Lugares II

a. estación de bomberos
b. comisaría
c. gasolinera
d. apartamentos
e. ciudad
f. campo
g. piscina, alberca
h. hospital
i. parque
j. fábrica
k. hotel
l. aeropuerto
m. salón de belleza
n. peluquería, barberia
o. estacionamiento
p. tienda

34. Profesiones

a. abogado
b. policía
c. carpintero
d. bombero
e. piloto
f. camarero, mesero
g. doctor, médico
h. enfermera
i. cartero
j. científico
k. arquitecto
l. granjero
m. cajero
n. carnicero
o. cocinero
p. barber, peluquero

35. Pasatiempos

a. muñeca
b. bate
c. pelota
d. pista
e. cuerda de brincar
f. radio
g. televisor
h. computadora
i. tocador de CDs
j. patines
k. patineta
l. raqueta
m. esquis
n. palo de golf
o. caña de pescar
p. pesas

36. Transportación

a. carro, coche
b. aeroplano
c. camión, autobús
d. tren
e. motocicleta
f. bicicleta
g. nave
h. barco, bote
i. camino
j. vías ferroviarias
k. letrero
l. luz delantera, faro
m. llanta ponchada
n. asiento
o. cinturón de seguridad
p. casco

1. Expressions 1

a. bon après-midi

b. bonjour

c. bon soir

d. a tes souhaits

e. quel est ton nom ?

f. mon nom est

g. bonjour

h. au revoir

i. s'il te plait

j. merci

k. fait attention

l. j'aime

m. je ne sais pas

n. je sais

o. je suis désolé

p. je suis désolé

2. Expressions 2

a. Laisse-moi presenter.

b. Enchanté

c. Quelle heure est-il ?

d. Il est …heures

e. Quel est la date d'aujoud'hu

f. Il est le 4 juillet

g. Quel âge as-tu ?

h. J'ai…ans

i. Quel temps fait-il ?

j. Combien ça coûte ?

k. Je ne comprends pas

l. Je suis gèné

m. J'ai faim

n. J'ai soif

o. J'ai peur

p. J'ai sommeil

3. Numéros 1

a. un

b. deux

c. trois

d. quatre

e. cinq

f. six

g. sept

h. huit

i. neuf

j. dix

k. onze

l. douze

m. treize

n. quatorze

o. quinze

p. sieze

4. Numéros 2

a. dix-sept

b. dix-huit

c. dix-neuf

d. vingt

e. trente

f. quarante

g. cinquante

h. soixante

i. soixante-dix

j. quatre-vingt

k. quatre-vingt-dix

l. cent

m. zéro

n. un demi

o. un tiers

p. un quart

5. Coloeurs

a. rouge

b. blanc

c. jaune

d. vert

e. bleu

f. violet

g. orange

h. marron

i. noir

j. fatigué

k. pressé

l. amoureux

m. surpris

n. en colère

o. ennuyé

p. amusé

6. Pronoms et Symboles

a. je

b. tu

c. vous

d. il

e. elle

f. nous

g. vous

h. ils

i. elles

j. vous

k. question

l. négation

m. passé

n. passé

o. présent

p. présent progressif

7. Verbes 1

a. se lever

b. s'asseoi

c. tourner

d. sauter

e. danser

f. chanter

g. pleurer

h. rire

i. ouvrir

j. ouvrir

k. ouvrir

l. ouvrir

m. lancer

n. jouer

o. mancher

p. courir

8. Verbes 2

a. lire

b. écrire

c. découper

d. dessiner

e. peindre

f. coller

g. étudier

h. écouter

i. parler

j. porter

k. ramasser

l. pouser

m. penser

n. savoir

o. se demander

p. répondre

9. Verbes 3

a. manger

b. boire

c. cuisiner

d. laver

e. laver

f. se laver

g. dormir

h. se brosser les cheveux

i. se coucher

j. se lever

k. regarder

l. s'habiller

m. enlever

n. mettre

o. se brosser les dents

p. pour relâcher

10. Verbes 4

a. gagner

b. perdre

c. trouver

d. chercher

e. laisser tomber

f. tomber

g. détruire

h. se cacher

i. casser

j. nager

k. monter

l. taper

m. blesser

n. glisser

o. se balancer

p. creuser

11. Verbes 5	12. Verbes 6	13. Verbes 7	14. Prépositions d'endroit	15. Adjectifs 1
a. toucher	a. vendre	a. conduire	a. dans	a. gentil
b. voir	b. acheter	b. écraser	b. hors	b. méchant
c. naître	c. payer	c. aller	c. en haut	c. fort
d. sentir	d. vouloir	d. retourner	d. en bas	d. faible
e. sourire	e. fabriquer	e. avoir besoin	e. devant	e. malade
f. mordre	f. porter	f. voyagerf.	f. dernière	f. en forme
g. griffer	g. donner	g. prendre	g. à droit	g. heureux
h. cueillir	h. parler	h. venir	h. à gauche	h. triste
i. pousser	i. déchirer	i. descendre	i. autour	i. gros
j. ramper	j. travailler	j. se lever	j. sur	j. maigre
k. voler	k. se battre	k. partir	k. sous	k. grand (haut)
l. écouter	l. s'arrêter	l. porter	l. au milieu	l. petit(bas)
m. nourrir	m.remplir	m. attendre	m. près de	m. laid
n. arroser	n. tourner	n. mettre	n. à travers	n. beau/belle
o. aimer	o. suivre	o. pousser	o. près	o. grand
p. embrasser	p. faire du vèlo	p. tirer	p. loin	p. petit

16. Adjectifs 3	17. Adjectifs 3	18.École	19. Corps	20. Vêtements
a. ouvert	a. chaud	a. professeur	a. jambe	a. robe
b. fermé	b. f roid	b. élève	b. pied	b. jupe
c. propre	c. endormi	c. table	c. visage	c. chemisier
d. sale	d. éveillé	d. chaise	d. cou	d. chemise
e. rapide	e. fatigué	e. bureau	e. doigt	e. bureau
f. lent	f. fou	f. porte	f. cheveux	f. tennis
g. stupide	g. pouirri	g. fenêtre	g. main	g. bottes
h. intelligent	h. frais	h. tableau	h. bras	h. chaussettes
i. frisé	i. lumineux	i. craie	i. dos	i. veste
j. raide	j. sombre	j. crayon	j. ventre	j. gants
k. long	k.riche	k. ciseau	k. poitrine	k. chapeau
l. court	l. pauvre	l. gomme	l. oeil	l. ceinture
m. près	m. plein	m. livre	m. tête	m. pull
n. loin	n. vide	n. papier	n. nez	n. costume
o. nouveau	o. humide	o. stylo	o. bouche	o. cravate
p. vieux	p. sec	p. cahier	p. oreille	p. casquette

21. Famille

a. famille
b. mère
c. père
d. fils
e. fille
f. frère
g. sœur
h. sœur
i. grand-père
j. oncle
k. tante
l. cousins
m. homme
n. femme
o. garçon
p. fille

22. Maison

a. cuisine
b. salle de bain
c. chambre
d. salon
e. lit
f. couverture
g. table
h. commode
i. garage
j. sous-sol
k. balcon
l. terrasse
m. cuisinière
n. escalier
o. cheminée
p. toit

23. Temps

a. pluie
b. il pleut
c. neiger
d. il neige
e. vent
f. il fait du vent
g. soleil
h. il fait du soleil
i. nuage
j. c'est nuageux
k. Jai chaud
l. Jai froid
m. ciel
n. étoiles
o. lune
p. thermomètre

24. Nourriturre 1

a. riz
b. spaghettis
c. jambon
d. viande
e. poisson
f. poulet
g. soupe
h. sandwich
i. pain
j. fromage
k. œuf
l. beurre
m. céréales
n. céréales
o. sel
p. bonbons

25. Nourriture 2

a. gâteau
b. biscuits
c. glace
d. jus d'orange
e. lait
f. boisson gazeuse
g. glace
h. pâte á mâcher
i. cacahuète
j. hot-dog
k. hamburger
l. f rites
m. bistec
n. confiture
o. beurre de cacahuète
p. ketchup

26. Fruit

a. fraise
b. raison
c. orange
d. pomme
e. cerise
f. citron
g. pastèque
h. pamplemousse
i. anana
j. poires
k. banane
l. noie de coco
m. framboise
n. datte
o. tomate
p. fruit

27. Légumes

a. carrottes
b. maïs
c. tomate
d. salade
e. celeries
f. courgette
g. broccolis
h. chou-fleur
i. pois
j. oignon
k. pomme de terre
l. potiron
m. concombre
n. piment
o. champignon
p. haricot

28 . Nature

a. mer
b. rivière
c. lac
d. l'herbe
e. montagne
f. arc-en-ciel
g. fleur
h. arbre
i. roches
j. boue
k. sable
l. île
m. feuille
n. branche
o. racine
p. mauvaise herbe

29. Animaux

a. souris
b. chèvre
c. coq
d. cochon
e. oiseau
f. cheval
g. poule
h. dinde
i. chat
j. lapin
k. canard
l. mouche
m. poisson
n. chien
o. mouton
p. vache

30. Animaux 2

a. serpent
b. tortue
c. ours
d. cerf
e. écureuil
f. loup
g. chouette
h. araignée
i. porc-épic
j. putois
k. raton-laveur
l. papillon
m. fourmi
n. abeille
o. renard
p. grenouille

31. Animaux 3

a. zèbre
b. chameau
c. singe
d. tigre
e. éléphant
f. lion
g. crocodile
h. girafe
i. pieuvre
j. requin
k. baleine
l. chauve-souris
m. dinosaure
n. phoque
o. kangourou
p. dauphin

32. Endroits 1

a. forêt
b. jungle
c. ferme
d. plage
e. banque
f. musée
g. école
h. église
i. désert
j. poste
k. restaurant
l. cinéma
m. bibliothèque
n. zoo
o. cirque
p. maison

33. Endroits 2

a. poste de pompiers
b. poste de police
c. station service
d. appartement
e. appartement
f. campagne
g. piscine
h. hôpital
i. jardin public
j. usine
k. hôtel
l. aéroport
m. salon de beauté
n. coiffeur
o. parking
p. magazins

34. Professions

a. avocat
b. policier
c. charpentier
d. pompier
e. pilote
f. serveur
g. docteur
h. infirmière
i. postier
j. scientifique
k. architecte
l. fermier
m. caissiére
n. boucher
o. chef cuisinier
p. coiffeur

35. Passe-temps

a. poupée
b. bat
c. balle
d. course
e. saut à la corde
f. radio
g. télévision
h. ordinateur
i. CD player
j. patins àroulettes
k. planche à roulettes
l. raquette
m. skis
n. club de golf
o. ranne à pèche
p. poids

36. Transport

a. voiture
b. avion
c. autobus
d. train
e. motocyclette
f. vélo
g. ravire
h. bateau
i. route
j. voie ferrée
k. panneaux
l. fermier
m. caissière
n. boucher
o. chef cuisinier
p. coiffeur

1. 短语 一

A.早上好
B.下午好
C.晚上好
D.祝福你
E.你叫什么？
F.我叫。。。
G.你好
H.再见
I.请
J.谢谢你
K.小心
L.我喜欢
M.我不知道
N.我知道
O.对不起
P.打扰一下

3。数字 一

A.一
B.二
C.三
D.四
E.五
F.六
G.七
H.八
I.九
J.十
K.十一
L.十二
M.十三
N.十四
O.十五
P.十六

5。颜色和形容

A.红色
B.白色
C.黄色
D.绿色
E.蓝色
F.紫色
G.橙色
H.褐色
I.黑色
J.累的
K.匆忙的
L.爱中
M.吃惊的
N.生气的
O.无聊的
P.滑稽的

7。动词 一

A.起立
B.坐下
C.转身
D.跳跃
E.跳舞
F.唱歌
G.哭泣
H.大笑
I.打开
J.关闭
K.踢
L.抓
M.扔
N.玩
O.走
P..跑

9。动词 三

A.吃
B.喝
C.煮
D.洗
E.打扫
F.用水洗
G 睡觉
H.梳发
I.上床
J.起床
K.看，看着
L.穿衣
M.脱下
N.穿上
O.刷牙
P.休息

2. 短语 二

A.让我介绍你
B.高兴认识你
C.现在什么时间？
D.现在----点钟
E.今天什么日子？
F.七月四号
G.你多大了？
H.我（6）岁。
I.天气怎样？
J.这个多少钱？
K.我不明白。
L.我很尴尬。
M.我饿了。
N.我渴了。
O.我害怕。
P.我很困。

4。数字 二

A.十七
B.十八
C.十九
D.二十
E. 三十
F.四十
G.五十
H.六十
I.七十
J. 八十
K.九十
L.一百
M.零
N.二分之一
O.三分之一
P.四分之一

6。代词和符号

A.我
B.你
C.您
D.他
E.她
F.我们
G.我们
H.他们
I.她们
J.你们

8。动词 二

A.读
B.写
C.剪
D.画
E.漆
F.粘贴
G.学习
H.听
I.讲，说
J.带走，携带
K.拿起
L.拿开
M.思考
N.知道
O..问
P.回答

10。动词 四

A.赢
B.输
C.找到
D.寻找
E.落下
F.倒下
G.击倒
H.藏
I.破坏
J.游泳
K..骑
L.击
M.受伤
N.滑行
O.摇摆
P.掘（地）

11.动词 五

A.触碰
B.看到
C.出生
D.闻到
E.微笑
F.咬人
G.挠痒
H.摘取
I.生长
J.爬行
K.飞行
L.听到，听
M.喂养
N.浇水
O.爱上
P.亲吻

13.动词 七

A.开车
B.碰撞
C.走
D.回去
E.需要
F.旅行
G.带走，携带
H.来
I.上去
J.下来
K.离开
L.带来
M.等待
N.放
O.推
P.拉

15。形容词 一

A.好的
B.坏的
C.强的
D.弱的
E.病的
F.健康的
G.快乐的
H.伤心的
I.胖的
J.瘦的
K.高的
L.矮的
M.丑的
N.漂亮的
O.大的
P.小的

17。形容词 三

A.热的
B.冷的
C.睡着的
D.醒着的
E.累的
F.疯的
G.腐烂的
H.新鲜的
I.明亮的
J.黑暗的
K.富的
L.穷的
M.满的
N.空的
O.湿的
P.干的

12。动词 六

A.卖
B.买
C.付钱
D.想要
E.做
F.携带
G.给
H.讲话
I.流泪
J.工作
K.打架
L.停车
M.填满
N.转身
O.跟随
P.骑

14。地方介词

A.里
B.出（对）
C.上
D.下
E.在前面
F.在后面，后面
G.（于）右
H.（于）左
I.周围
J.上，上面的
K.下，底下
L.在中间，之间
M.相邻
N.穿过
O/接近，靠近
P.远

16。形容词 二

A. 开着的
B. 关着的
C.干净的
D.脏的
E. 快的
F.慢的
G.笨的
H.聪明的
I.有卷发的
J. 直的
K.长的
L.短的
M.近的
N.远的
O.新的
P.旧的

18。学校

A.老师
B．学生
C.桌子
D.椅子
E.课桌
F.门
G.窗子
H.黑板
I.粉笔
J. 铅笔
K.剪刀
L.l橡皮
M. 书
N. 纸
O.钢笔
P.笔记本

19. 身体

A. 腿
B. 脚
C. 脸
D. 脖子
E. 手指
F. 头发
G. 手
H. 手臂
I. 背
J. 胃
K. 胸前
L. 眼睛
M. 头
N. 鼻子
O. 嘴
P. 耳朵

21. 家庭

A. 家人
B. 妈妈
C. 爸爸
D. 儿子
E. 女儿
F. 兄弟
G. 姐妹
H. 外婆，奶奶
I. 外公，爷爷
J. 叔叔
K. 阿姨
L. 堂兄弟
M. 男人
N. 女人
O. 男孩
P. 女孩

23。天气

A. 下雨
B. 正在下雨
C. 下雪
D. 正在下雪
E. 刮风
F. 在刮风
G. 太阳
H. 晴天
I. 云
J. 阴天
K. 热天
L. 冷天
M. 天空
N. 星星
O. 月亮
P. 温度计

25。食物

A. 蛋糕
B. 饼干
C. 冰淇淋
D. 果汁
E. 牛奶
F. 爆米花
G. 冰
H. 口香糖
I. 花生
J. 热狗
K. 汉堡包
L. 薯条
M. 牛排
N. 果冻，果酱
O. 花生酱
P. 番茄酱

27蔬菜

A. 胡萝卜
B. 玉米
C. 萝卜
D. 莴苣
E. 芹菜
F. 南瓜小果
G. 绿菜花
H. 菜花
I. 豌豆
J. 洋葱
K. 土豆
L. 南瓜
M. 泡菜
N. 辣椒
O. 蘑菇
P. 蘑菇

20。衣服

A. 长裙
B. 短裙
C. 短上衣
D. 衬衫
E. 裤子
F. 鞋子
G. 靴子
H. 袜子
I. 外套
J. 手套
K. 帽子
L. 腰带
M. 毛衣
N. 西装
O. 领带
P. 便帽

22。房子

A. 厨房
B. 浴室
C. 卧室
D. 客厅
E. 床
F. 小地毯
G. 饭厅
H. 食具橱
I. 车库
J. 地下室
K. 阳台
L. 露台
M. 炉子
N. 楼梯
O. 烟囱
P. 屋顶

24。食物 一

A. 米饭
B. 面条
C. 火腿
D. 肉
E. 鱼
F. 鸡肉
G. 汤
H. 三明治
I. 面包
J. 芝士
K. 蛋
L. 黄油
M. 壳类食物
N. 糖
O. 盐
P. 糖果

26。水果

A. 草莓
B. 葡萄
C. 橘子
D. 苹果
E. 樱桃
F. 柠檬
G. 西瓜
H. 柚子
I. 菠萝
J. 梨
K. 香蕉
L. 椰子
M. 树莓
N. 芒果
O. 西红柿
P. 果

28. 自然

A. 大海
B. 河流
C. 湖
D. 草
E. 山
F. 彩虹
G. 花
H. 树
I. 石头
J. 泥
K. 沙
L. 岛
M. 叶
N. 根
O. 根
P. 杂草

29．动物 一
A. 老鼠
B. 山羊
C. 公鸡
D. 猪
E. 鸟
F. 马
G. 母鸡
H. 火鸡
I. 猫
J. 兔子
K. 鸭
L. 苍蝇
M. 鱼
N. 狗
O. 羊
P. 奶牛

30。动物 二
A. 蛇
B. 龟
C. 熊
D. 鹿
E. 松鼠
F. 狼
G. 猫头鹰
H. 蜘蛛
I. 豪猪
J. 北美臭
K. 浣熊
L. 蝴蝶
M. 蚂蚁
N. 蜜蜂
O. 狐狸
P. 青蛙

31.动物Ⅲ
A.斑马
B.骆驼
C.猴
D.虎
E.大象
F狮子
G.鳄鱼
H.长颈鹿
I.章鱼
J.鲨鱼
K.鲸
L.蝙蝠
M.恐龙
N.海豹
O.袋鼠
P.海豚

32.地点I
A.森林，木材
B.丛林
C.农场
D.海滩
E.银行
F.博物馆
G.学校
H.教堂
I.沙漠
J.邮局
K.餐厅
L.电影院
M.图书馆
N.动物园
O.马戏团
P.房子

33.地点Ⅱ
A.消防局
B.派出所
C加油站
D.公寓
E.城市
F.国家
G.游泳池
H.医院
I.公园
J.工厂
K.酒店
L.机场
M.美容院
N.理发店
O.停车场
P.商店

34.专业
A.律师
B.警察
C.木匠
D.消防员
E.飞行员
F.服务员
G.医生
H.护士
I.邮递员
J.科学家
K.建筑师
L.农民
M.收银员
N.屠夫
O.主厨，厨师
P.理发师

35.消遣
A.娃娃
B.球棒
C.球
D.跑道
E.跳绳
F.广播电台
G.电视
H.计算机(电脑)
I.CD播放机
J.溜冰鞋
K.滑板
L.球拍
M.滑雪板
N.高尔夫球棒
O.鱼竿
P.举重

36.交通运输
A.汽车
B.飞机
C.巴士
D.火车
E.摩托车
F.自行车
G.小船
H.大船,舰
I.道路
J.火车轨道
K.标志
l.头灯
M.爆胎
N.座位
O.安全带
P.头盔

Key- Arabic

5.الوان	4.ارقام	3.ارقام	2. التعبـــيرات	1.1 التعبـــيرات
a. احمر	a. عشر سبعة	a. واحد	a.اعرفك ان لي حاسم	a. صبـاح الخـير
b. ابيض	b. ثمانيـة عشر	b. اثنين	b.تسـرفت بمعرفتـك	b. مساء الخـير
c. اصفر	c. عشر تسعة	c. ثلاثة	c.الوقـت هو ما	c. الخـير مساء
d. اخضر	d. عشرون	d. اربعة	d.انها الساعة	d. صحا
e. ازرق	e. ثلاثـون	e. خمسة	e.اليـوم تـاريخ هو ما	e. ما اسمك؟
f. ارجواني	f. اربعون	f. ستة	f.انه الرابـه من تموز	f. اسمي هو
g. برتقـالي	g. خمسون	g. سبعة	g.العكر من تبلـغ كم	g. عليكـم السـلام
h. بـني	h. ستون	h. ثمانية	ان فـي السادسـة من عمري	h. السـلامة مغ
i. اسود	i. سبعون	i. تسـعة	h.	i. فضـلك من
j. متعب	j. ثمانون	j. عشرة	i.الطقس كيف حاله	j. لك شكـرا
k. عجلة في	k. تسعون	k. عشر احد	j.هذا هو طم	k. احذر. انتيـه
l. الحب فـي	l. مئـة	l. عشر اثنـا	k.افهـم لا انا	l. اود
m. فاجأ	m. صفـر	m. عشر ثلاثـة	l.بـالحرج اسعر انا	m. اعرف لا أنا
n. غاضب	n. نصف	n. عشر اربعة	m.انـا جـائع	n. اعرف أنا
o. ملل	o. ثلث	o. عشر خمسة	n. انا	o. اسف انا
p. مضحك. مسل	p. ريـع	p. عشر ستة	o.خاءف انا	p. اعـذرني
			p.انـا نعسـان	

10.الافعـــال	9.الافعـــال	8.الافعـــال	7.الافعـــال	6.ر الضـمائ
a. ربـح	a. اكل	a. قرأ	a. نهض	انظر الـى رقم 37
b. خسر	b. شرب	b. كتـب	b. جلس	a.
c. وجد	c. طها	c. قطع	c. انعطف	b.
d. بحـث	d. غسـل	d. رسم	d. قفـز	c.
e. تـرك	e. نظف	e. لـون	e. رقص	d.
f. سقط	f. استحم	f. لصق	f. غنـى	e.
g. تغلـب	g. نام	g. درس	g. بكـى	f.
h. خبأ	h. مسط الشـعر	h. اسـتمع	h. ضحك	g.
i. تكسـر	i. الفـراش الـى اذهب	i. اقول .الكـلام	i. فتـح	
j. سبـح	j. نهض	j. نقل. اخرج	j. غلـق	
k. ركب	k. راقب	k. التقـط	k. ركل	
l. أصاب	l. لبـس	l. جاتبـا وضعه	l. بـه امسك	
m. أذى	m. خلـع	m. اعتقـد	m. رمى	
n. الانـزلق	n. ارتـدى	n. عرف	n. لعـب	
o. تمايـل .هز	o. اسنان فرشـاة	o. سأل	o. مشـى	
p. حفـر	p. استرخى	p. أجاب	p. ركض	

11.الافعال
a. لمس
b. رأى
c. ان يولد
d. شم
e. مابتس
f. عض
g. شطب
h. التقط
i. كبر
j. زحف
k. طار
l. سمع .اصغى
m. اطعم
n. روى
o. حب
p. قبل

12.الافعال
a. باع
b. اشترى
c. دفع
d. اراد
e. احدث
f. نقل
g. اعطي
h. تكلم
i. قطع
j. عمل
k. حارب
l. اوقف السيارة
m. امتلا
n. استدار
o. تبع
p. ركب

13.الصفات
a. ساق .قاد
b. تحطم
c. ذهب
d. أرجع
e. أحتاج
f. سافر
g. اخذ .نقل
h. اتى
i. صعد
j. نزل
k. ترك
l. جلب
m. انتظر
n. وضع
o. دفع
p. سحب

14.الجر
a. في
b. خارج
c. فوق
d. ادنى
e. امام
f. موءخرة في
g. اليمين الى
h. اليسار الى
i. حول
j. فوق
k. تحت
l. منتصف في
m. قرب
n. خلال
o. قرب
p. بعيد

15.الصفات
a. جيد
b. رديئ
c. قوي
d. ضعيف
e. مريض
f. جيد
g. سعيد
h. حزين
i. سمين
j. رفيع
k. طويل
l. قصير
m. قبيح
n. جميل
o. ضخم
p. صغير

16.الصفات
a. مفتوح
b. مغلق
c. نظيف
d. متسخ
e. سريع
f. بطيئ
g. تافه
h. ذكي
i. الشعر جعد
j. مستقيم
k. طويل
l. قصير
m. قريب
n. بعيد
o. جديد
p. قديم

17.الصفات
a. ساخن
b. بارد
c. نائم
d. يقظ
e. عبثت
f. مجنون
g. فاسد
h. طازج
i. ساطع
j. معتم
k. غني
l. فقير
m. ملئ
n. فارغ
o. رطب
p. جاف

18.المدرسة
a. معلم
b. طالب
c. طاولة
d. كرسي
e. مكتب
f. باب
g. نافذة
h. لوح
i. طبشورة
j. رصاص قلم
k. مقص
l. ممحاة
m. كتاب
n. ورقة
o. قلم
p. مذكرة

19.الجسم
a. ساق
b. قدم
c. وجه
d. رقبة
e. اصبع
f. شعر
g. يد
h. ذراع
i. ظهر
j. معدة
k. صدر
l. نعي
m. راس
n. أنف
o. فم
p. أذن ا

20.الملابس
a. فستان
b. تنورة
c. بلوزة
d. قميص
e. سروال
f. احذية
g. طويلة احذية
h. جوارب
i. معطف
j. قفاز
k. قبعة
l. حزام
m. سترة
n. بذلة
o. عنق ربطة
p. قبعة

21.العائلة
a. عائلة
b. ام
c. اب
d. ابن
e. ابنة
f. اخ
g. اخت
h. جدة
i. جد
j. العم
k. العمة
l. العم ابناء
m. رجل
n. امراة
o. ولد
p. فتاة

22.البيت
a. مطبخ
b. حمام
c. غرفة نوم
d. غرفة جلوس
e. مضجع
f. سجادة
g. غرفة طعام
h. خزانة
i. مراب
j. طابق ارضي
k. شرفة
l. باحة مرصوفة
m. موقد
n. سلالم
o. مدخنة
p. سقف

23.الطقس
a. مطر
b. انها تمطر
c. ثلج
d. انها تثلج
e. رياح
f. انه عاصف
g. شمس
h. انها مشمس
i. سحابة
j. انها غائمة
k. حار انه
l. انه بارد
m. سماء
n. نجوم
o. قمر
p. الحرارة ميزان

24.الطعام
a. ارز
b. شعيرية
c. الخنزير لحم
d. لحمة
e. سمك
f. دجاج
g. ساحح
h. عروس
i. خبز
j. جبنة
k. بيض
l. زبدة
m. حبوب
n. سكر
o. ملح
p. حلوى

25.الطعام
a. كعكة
b. بسكويت
c. بوظة
d. عصير
e. حليب
f. فوار شراب
g. جليد
h. علكة
i. فستق
j. نقانق
k. لحم سطيرة
l. بطاطا مقلية
m. بفتاك
n. مربى
o. الفستق زبدة
p. الصلصة

26.الفواكه
a. فراولة
b. عنب
c. برتقال
d. تقاح
e. كرز
f. ليمون حامض
g. بطيخ
h. ليمون الجنة
i. اناناس
j. اجاص
k. موز
l. جوز الهند
m. توت
n. تمر
o. طماطم
p. فاكهة

27.الخضار
a. جزر
b. ذرة
c. لفت
d. خس
e. كرفس
f. كوسى
g. احضر نبيطقر
h. قرنبيط
i. بازيلاء
j. بصل
k. بطاطا
l. يقطين
m. مخلل
n. حار فلفل
o. فطر
p. خضراء فاصوليا

28.الطبيعة
a. محيط .بحر
b. النهر
c. بحيرة
d. العشب
e. الجبال
f. قزح قوس
g. زهرة
h. شجرة
i. الصخور
j. الطين
k. الرمال
l. الجزيرة
m. نبات ورقة
n. فرع
o. جذور
p. الاعشاب

29.حيوانات
a. الفأر
b. ماعز
c. ديك
d. خنزير
e. عصفور
f. حصان
g. دجاجة
h. حبش
i. قطة
j. ارنب
k. بطة
l. يطير
m. سمك
n. كلب
o. خراف
p. بقرة

30.حيوانات
a. ثعبان
b. سلحفاة
c. دب
d. غزال
e. سنجاب
f. ذئب
g. بومة
h. عنكبوت
i. النيص
j. ظربان
k. الراكون
l. فراشة
m. النمل
n. النحلة
o. ثعلب
p. ضفدع

31.حيوانـات

a. حمار وحشي
b. جمل
c. قرد
d. نمر
e. فيـل
f. اسد
g. تمسـاح
h. زرافة
i. اخطبـوط
j. قرش
k. حوت
l. خفـاش
m. حيوان منقرض
n. مهر
o. كنغـر
p. دلفيـن

32.اماكن

a. غابـات
b. ادغال
c. مزرعة
d. شاطئ
e. بنـك
f. متحف
g. مدرسة
h. كنيسـة
i. صحراء
j. مكتـب البريـد
k. مطعم
l. افـلام
m. مكتبـة
n. حديقة الحيوانـات
o. سـيرك
p. منزل

33.اماكن

a. اطفائيـة
b. مركز للشـرطة
c. محطة وقود
d. شـقق
e. مدينـة
f. بلـد
g. بركـة للسـباحة
h. مستشـفى
i. حديقة
j. معمل
k. فندق
l. مطار
m. صـالون تجميـل
n. صـالون حلاقـة
o. موقف للسـيارات
p. مخزن

34.المهن

a. محام
b. شرطي
c. نجـار
d. مقاتـل النار
e. طيـار
f. نـادل
g. طبيـب
h. ممرضة
i. ساعي بريـد
j. عالمة
k. مهندس معماري
l. مزارع
m. صـراف
n. جزار
o. طاه
p. حلاق

35.سـليتَ

a. دميـة
b. عجينـة
c. كرة
d. يتعقـب
e. على القفـز
f. راديـو
g. تلفـزيـون
h. العقـل الالكـتروني
i. جهاز الكـتروني
j. مزلجات
k. لوح التـزلج
l. مضرب
m. الزحافـات
n. نادي الغولـف
o. قصبة الصـيد
p. الاوزان

36.النقـل

a. سـيارة
b. طـائرة
c. حافلـة
d. قطـار
e. دراجة ناريـة
f. دراجة هوائيـة
g. سـفينة
h. زورق
i. طريق
j. السـكك الحديدية
j. اشارات
l. المصـابيح الامامية
m. اطار مثقـوب
n. مقعـد
o. حزام الامان
p. الخوذة

37.الضـمائر

a. انا
b. نحن
c. انتَ
d. انتما
e. انتم
f. انتِ
g. انتما
h. انتنَّ
i. هو
j. هما
k. هم
l. هي
m. هما
n. هنَّ

Suggested Uses for Perfect Pics

1. **BIG FLASHCARDS**- Enlarge the pictures to the desired size via overheard or opaque projector, or use copier. Put onto cardstock (for strength) and color, if you want.

    A. **TEACH- REVIEW**

    Object: To teach or review vocabulary in big or small group.

    Procedure: Show each card as you say the word. Have students repeat.

    Variation: Students pair off, each group with a set of small cards.

    B. **AROUND THE WORLD**

    Object: To quickly and correctly name the cards.

    Procedure: Ask two students who sit next to each other to stand up. Show both of them a previously hidden card. The first one to correctly name the card wins, and he moves on to the next student. The student continues until he loses, at which time he sits down in the victor's seat. The winner is the student that travels the farthest, hopefully all **around the class (world).**

    C. **MODIFIED TPR (Some cards lend themselves to modified physical** response to your command, but not all of them.)

    Object: To respond to commands given in the target language.

    Procedure: After reviewing the cards, place them around the room. Tell the students, "Go to the (library, restaurant)", "Where are you going?" "I'm going to the (library, restaurant). "Where is he?" "He's at the (library, restaurant). Continue with other cards.

    D. **SENTENCE BUILDING**

    Object: To teach or review vocabulary, sentence structure, grammar; and to have students gain valuable oral or written practice "reading' or "decoding" these "sentences".

    Procedure: Arrange cards into the desired position on the chalkboard rail (or ask some students to hold them for you in the front of the class.)

    FOR VERB CONJUGATING:

Present	I	see.
Past	You	talk.
Future	He	sings.

    FOR ADJECTIVES:

The man	sees	(the) red	book.

2.TALKING CARDS: Bell and howell and other companies make Language Master Cards, or some variation of long blank card with a magnetic strip for your voice or the students'.

Object: To hear, see and read the new vocabulary at the same time.

Procedure: Glue, tape, or paper clip the pictures and the written word to a card. Then record the correct pronunciation on the same card. Use these cards for catching up absent or slower students, or independent learners.

Variation: Have the students record their voices on the cards as a test.

3. **FISH** (For younger children) See PATTERNS

Object: To retrieve the specified fish.

Procedure: Cut out the shapes for as many fish as you need and glue a picture on it. Attach a paper clip to the fish. Using a fishing pole made of a pencil, string and any small magnet, tell student to fish, or give you "restaurant/doctor" or whatever.

4. **GO FISH** (For groups of 2-4)

Object: To review misc. vocabulary.

Procedure: Make four copies of the desired vocabulary page. Paste the 64 pics onto index cards, and draw four different shapes, colors or traditional suits on them.

(A red bee, a square bee, a bee of clovers…) Play in the traditional way.

5. **MEMORY OR CONCENTRATION** (For readers, beginners or better.)

Object: To improve the recall of vocabulary (written and pictured)

Procedure: cut index cards in half. Glue a picture on one half, and write the word on the other. Mix up, put the cards face down in four rows of eight. Each student tries to get pairs by guessing or remembering where the cards are.

Variation: For a large class, use whole index cards for the pics and words. Make a large poster board with library pockets with numbers on them. The class is divided into two teams. One student pre team chooses two numbers and the teacher takes them out to see of it's a match. Each team receives a point for their match.

6. **TPR (Total Physical Response)**

Object: To give and response to the correct command.

Procedure: Give the students verb cards (or other cards as well for more challenge)

Have one student correctly command another according to the picture they have.

7. **SPINNER (See PATTERNS)**

Object: To quickly and correctly name vocabulary.

Procedure; Divide any bug cardstock circle or pizza circle into eights or more, and glue pics in each section by the edge of the circle, Secure a spinner with a brad so that it spins around easily. Take turns spinning the spinner. The first person to correctly name the pictures gets to do the next spin.

Variation: Make a circle as above, make overhead and play with the whole class.

8. **DICE (See PATTERNS)**

Object: To quickly and correctly name the vocabulary.

Procedure: Using the pattern for the die, glue six pics on each face and copy. (If you can, copy onto cardstock.) Fold the die and tape together with wide tape. Throw the die gently and see who can correctly name the pic. The winner gets to gently it.

Variation: Use a big foam die and use straight pins to secure the pics. Of course it is not recommended to do this with young children.

9. **WHEELS (See PATTERNS)**

Object: To correctly decode or say what the wheels indicate.

Procedure: Make two and three different sized wheels, divided into eights, with pic glued onto the edges. You or the students move the wheels to make logical or interesting sentences.

Variation: Make the wheels on an overheard for large class participation.

10. **CALENDAR (See PATTERNS)**

Object: To review the days and other vocabulary by sentences building.

Procedure: Get a big poster board, divide into squares (7 x ?) as seen in the pattern.

Put gummed magnet strip (found at craft stores) in each square. Cut out rectangles of cardstock and write the days on them. (You might want to number them also, with Sunday bring 1, etc. Now cut out pics which have been copied or glued onto cardstock.

Attach a paper clip to each card. You make up a sentence (simple ones at first then gradually more complex) and have the students "make" the sentences by placing the cards in the correct square. Ex: On Monday my aunt dances. On Tuesday my brother sleeps. Etc. Have the students "read" the sentences back to you, a day at a time.

Variation: For a large class, make a calendar overheard. Use smaller than normal pics, cut into horizontal strips. Use an overheard marker pen to write in the days.

11. **BINGO** (Good for cooperative learning groups, big groups, pairs.) See PATTERNS

Object: To recognize and eventually name vocabulary.

Procedure: Make bingo boards by following the number grids in the PATTERN section. (Each number represents a certain pictures, you decide) Copy onto cardstock and leave as is or have students color a board for homework. The first time you play the game, show the card as you say the word. Later only say the word (no card). The next time student can't win unless he can recite all the word that were in his winning line. Next time (if you're not tired of the game yet) allude to the word, but don't actually say the word. Ex: I buy things there (store)

Variation: Have students read off the cards for small groups.

12. **SCAVENGER HUNT**

Object: to be able to match the written word with the pic.

Procedure: Give half the group pictures, and the other half the matching words.

When you say "go", the students get up and look for their "partner".

Variation: Whisper the word to each of the non-pictured group. This will test their oral recall which is a lot harder than the written word.

13. SENTENCE STRIPS AND BOARD (See PATTERNS)

Object: To make and "read" logical sentences.

Procedure: Make a 8/12 by 11 cardstock "sentence strip" board using the pattern as a model. Make hands for the clock, secure with a brad, cut the slits for the strips.

Make vertical strips of related pics (about 8 pics pre strip). Either tell the students what to "write" or they make sentences to "read" to the class or group. Variation: Use in Cooperative learning groups or pairs. See how many logical and correct sentences can be said or written in a specified time.

14. PICTURE STORIES

Object: To integrate the learned vocabulary and write stories.

Procedure: Provide the students with 10 or more small pics and writing paper.

Students individually, in pairs, or in groups write a picture story integrating the words with the pictures.

Ex. Everyday the and the their dinner in their

15. DETECTIVE/ SECRET CODES

Object: To decipher or communicate via pictures, and tell or write correctly.

Procedure: Write some sentences using the letter and page numbers of the pics. Have individuals or groups decipher your message or sentences. Make sure that they add the little important words not symbolized by pics. (The, and, to…) These may take form of worksheets or just something written on the broad. The students should have the necessary pages at their disposal. (Preferably a picture dictionary)

Ex: 1a + 9a + 9b + 21h + 22a = Good morning. I eat and drink in Grandma's kitchen.

16. GUESS WHO, WHAT

Object: To be able to describe pictures, and to understand the descriptions.

Procedure: Copy some of the pics on paper, cut out and tape to students' back. The students walk around and describe in the target language the pic on another's back.

Each student tries to guess what his picture is.

Variation: The students may ask yes-no question of other students.

17. PEOPLE SENTENCES (Good for a big room or an outside activity)

Object: To correctly make sentences with pictures according to directions. Procedure: The class is divided into two or three groups with each group having the same cards. Each student in the groups has at least one pictures, preferably big cardstock cards. The teacher calls out a sentence. The students have to hurry to form the sentence, each student holding the picture in front of him, and in the correct physical order. You might want one person per team to be the director. The first team to correctly form the pictures sentence gets a point.

Variation: This can be done inside and quietly if each student has many cards to form at his desk.

18. MASTERY LEARNING/INDIVIDUALIZATION

Object: To have the student learn as much as he can at his own speed.

Procedure: Make a big classroom chart with everyone's name on a vertical list, and the names of the pic topics (VERBS I, TRANSPORTATION, FAMILY...) on another horizontal list. Quiz students orally or on paper and if and when they get 90-100%

On a certain topic, put a sticker by their name. (For points or extra credit, and yes, this really works in high school)

Variation: Instead of a big group chart, each student has his own smaller chart where you put stickers if he qualifies. That way he competes only with himself.

The use for **PERFECT PICS** is really limitless. These ideas are only the tip of an iceberg. You and your students will come up with many more. Many of these ideas take a lot of time to prepare. There are many helpful students who would love to help you during lunch, after school, or even at home. It's hard to believe, but some students are actually bored at times! If the games or cards are laminated or covered with clear contact paper, they will last almost forever.

A KEY for the pics is provided although most of the time it won't be needed. Also, to you or to the student, the picture may look instead like something else. Either you may decide to disagree with what I had intended it to be (That's fine, Ill never know) or you many have to explain or clarify. Also, some pictures may be culturally different to some students, so we need to be careful of assumptions. (Church for a Muslim may look just like another building or many of the professions may be strange to others.)

Patterns and Examples

Dice Example

Dice Pattern

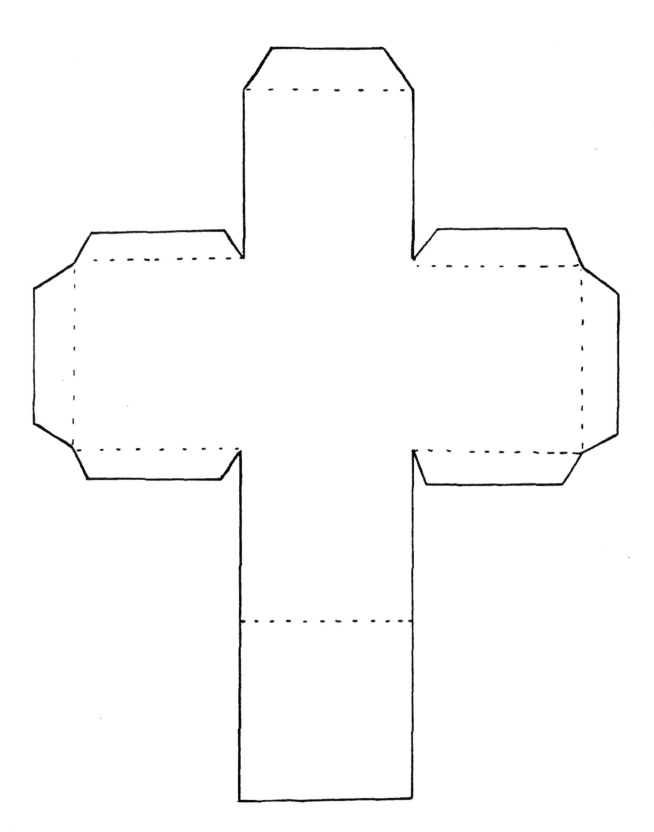

Spinner Sample

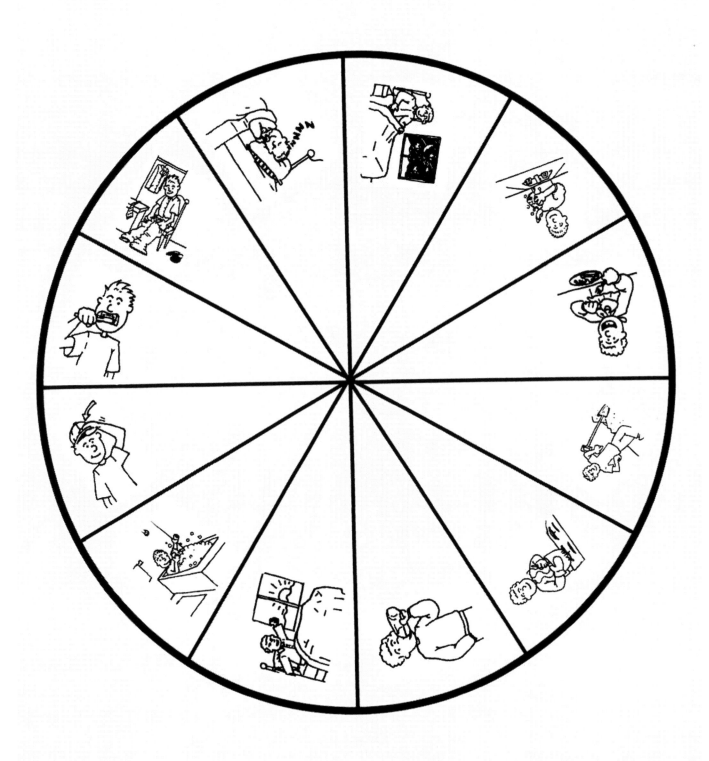

Small Secondary Spinner Sample

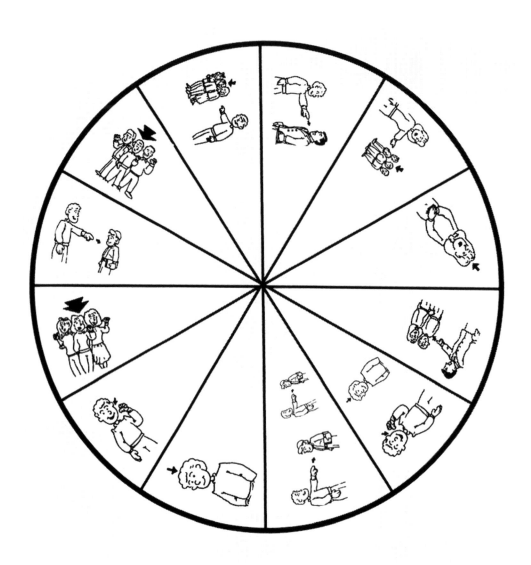

Spinner Pattern

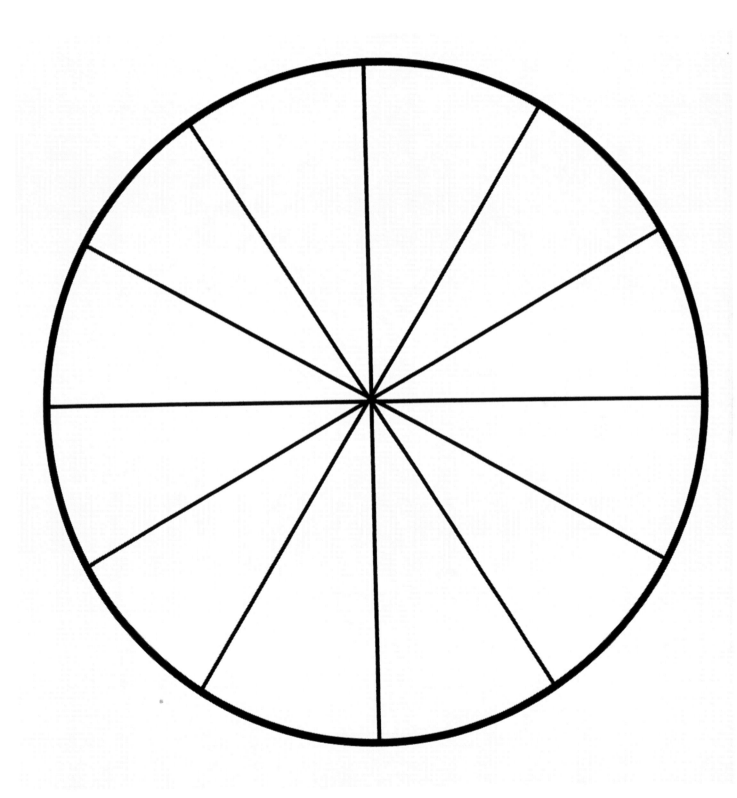

Small Secondary Spinner Pattern

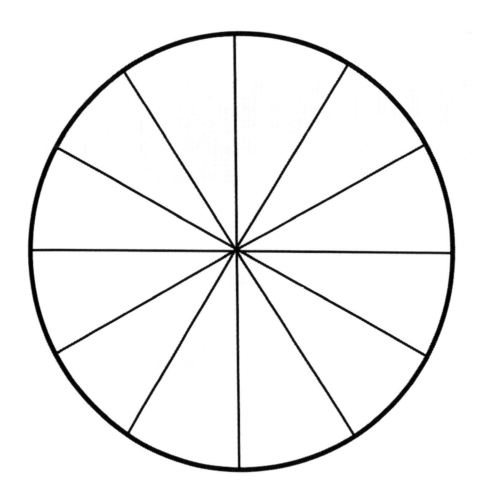

Visual Calendar

Sunday	Saturday	Friday	Thursday	Wednesday	Tuesday	Sunday
6:05	**4:15**	**9:30**	**10:45**	**1:25**	**8:10**	**3:00**

Sentence Strips Boards

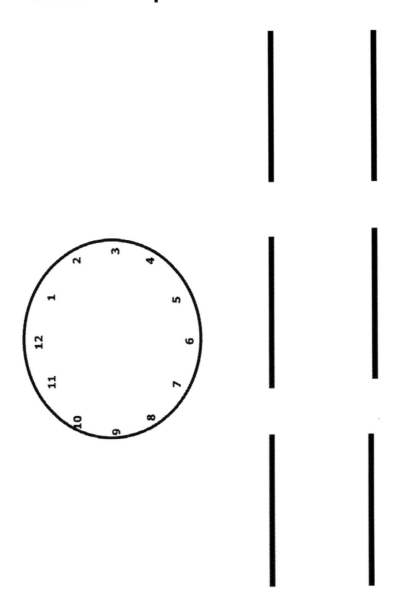

Verbs 1

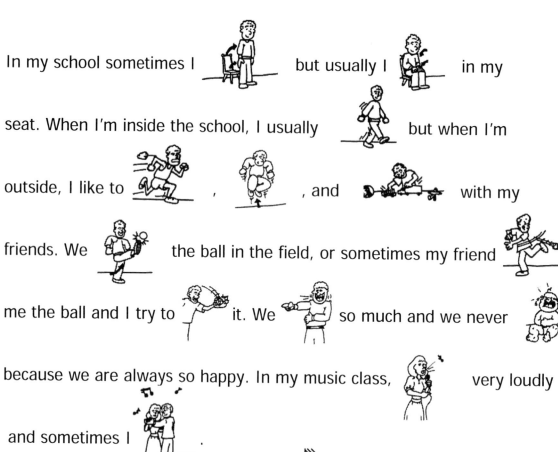

In my school sometimes I ___ but usually I ___ in my

seat. When I'm inside the school, I usually ___ but when I'm

outside, I like to ___ , ___ , and ___ with my

friends. We ___ the ball in the field, or sometimes my friend

me the ball and I try to ___ it. We ___ so much and we never

because we are always so happy. In my music class, ___ very loudly

and sometimes I ___ .

I am so excited every morning when I ___ my front door and leave for

school. In the afternoon when it's time to go home, I get a little sad when

I  the door behind me. I and wave to my

friends and my teacher. I'm very happy that I get to go to school

tomorrow, too!

Bingo Card (See following pages for guide)

Guides for Bingo Cards

31	4	25	14
7	29	19	22
18	9	17	10
6	8	21	28

3	9	25	23
10	17	30	5
13	19	4	26
24	32	27	11

31	27	21	18
11	9	13	5
2	20	26	7
25	24	10	12

30	12	25	29
10	14	8	13
32	21	17	27
22	23	24	18

17	27	23	5
9	14	26	10
28	1	20	19
25	7	13	31

30	29	3	5
32	21	11	1
6	23	12	22
9	20	13	14

32	7	16	23
12	17	5	3
13	20	4	26
29	14	27	24

19	27	7	23
1	8	18	26
17	4	15	20
31	16	6	10

23	18	9	1
14	3	4	17
7	12	26	2
22	32	27	19

23	24	32	17
21	5	26	18
8	27	4	22
19	20	25	11

7	23	28	22
1	20	31	5
8	9	27	18
30	15	6	25

30	7	18	2
12	14	5	13
19	20	28	26
27	1	8	21

23	24	32	17
21	5	26	18
8	27	4	22
19	20	25	11

7	23	28	22
1	20	31	5
8	9	27	18
30	15	6	25

30	7	18	2
12	14	5	13
19	20	28	26
27	1	8	21

1	22	3	4
6	26	29	17
14	25	31	20
15	30	10	27

18	29	5	26
27	28	2	15
22	8	11	3
24	19	31	1

2	30	13	14
4	5	19	21
32	28	9	29
11	20	15	27

13	20	21	25
1	2	5	12
29	9	22	10
24	17	27	8

25	4	17	26
11	31	15	29
3	23	27	5
20	30	7	2

29	11	27	28
32	14	19	21
1	26	31	24
13	22	8	15

32	5	4	29
7	1	2	31
26	19	31	10
8	9	18	6

13	30	5	32
26	7	19	12
3	31	15	18
24	11	14	21

32	1	29	16
6	7	15	8
9	14	22	11
20	4	31	28

15	11	32	20
13	7	16	28
17	18	19	1
21	9	24	29

8	16	12	15
3	22	27	19
4	10	18	20
9	32	1	30

20	26	14	8
18	5	11	25
3	2	15	31
10	9	21	7

28	20	31	11
5	21	3	13
17	22	19	23
8	29	18	4

3	25	22	1
5	7	29	6
12	28	19	18
32	2	4	8

16	18	31	30
2	29	19	3
24	15	13	12
4	25	1	8

Other Great Educational Materials by Lonnie Dai Zovi

Spanish ¡Alive! (booklet & CD) – 15 simple children's songs including Hokey Pokey, Buenos días, ¿Cómo te llamas? etc. Good for elementary classes and Spanish 1. Sold alone or part of set.

Español ¡Alegre! (booklet &CD) – 16 children's songs including songs about days, time, weather, school, food, etc. Good for all ages

Cantos, Ritmos, Y Rimas – (Bk & CD) An innovative approach to learning Spanish vocabulary, syntax and grammar through chants set to Caribbean rhythms. Appropriate for all ages but mostly 5th – 12th grades.

Cantiques, Rhymes, Et Rimes – (Bk & CD) An innovative approach to learning French vocabulary, syntax, and grammar through Cajun, Zydeco, and Haitian rhythms. Appropriate for all ages but mostly 5th – 12th grades.

Canti, Ritmi e Rime is an exciting, revolutionary way of teaching and reinforcing Italian through chants set to catchy tunes or penetrating beats. The chants teach both thematic topics (family, weather, house, body, countries and more) and also grammatical points such as commands, prepositions, object pronouns, past tense with *essere/avere* and verb conjugations. No 5th through 12th grade Italian class should be without this CD/Book combination. The Canti set includes CD, scripts of the 21 songs, cloze exercises, and more.

Cantos Calientes – (Bk & CD) More great chants for the classroom including por/para, preterite/imperfect, ser/estar and many subjunctive chants all set to Hispanic beats such as flamenco, salsa, andina, cumbia, vallenato and more.. Appropriate for Spanish 1-4.

Gira Musical – Extremely beautiful and colorful musical treasures from all over the Spanish-speaking world. Includes words and exercises.

Musical Arabic – An innovative CD/Book combination that pleasantly teaches and reinforces Modern Standard Arabic in a fun and non-threatening way. The book contains the scripts of the 22 lively chants, rhythms and songs (alphabet, birthday, family, countries, days, everyday expressions, possessives, simple verb conjugations, etc.) in both Arabic and phonetic (romanized) scripts for easier understanding by all students. There are many exercises that follow the lessons of the songs and also a picture glossary so that the learner may understand the songs without cumbersome translations. Good for all ages.

Rockin' Rhythms and Rhymes – (Workbook, Teacher's Guide & CD) A unique and innovative system of learning English through rhythmic recitations accompanied by music such as reggae, bluegrass, Irish jig, calypso, blues and much more. Grammar, vocabulary, and pronunciation stressed. Good for all ages.

Mariachi y Más – (Bk & CD) Indispensable music and workbook for intermediate, advanced, and bilingual classes. Mexico's 16 most beloved songs with scripts, cloze activities, worksheets, trivia, history, etc. Great AP tool.

Practice with Pics – Workbook to stimulate simple oral or written expressions using pictures. Any language, any level especially low literacy students.

Perfect Picture Stories – 36 picture stories in 6 frames similar to the AP test with stimulus questions, vocabulary and oral comprehension questions in Spanish, French and English (German on request)

Expression Bingo - A set of 34 big bingo cards of 36 different common expressions including *What's your name?, How much is that?, How old are you?* Pictures calling cards in Engl, Span, Fr, Germ, Jap, Chin, It, and Arabic

Accent on Art – Contains readings, exercises, maps, activities and more to teach/learn about 10 Mexican and Spanish artists; their lives, works and more. It is written in Spanish, which makes it applicable for the upper levels, or as a source book for teachers.

Muscal Echoing – Call and response musical and pictorial program that permanently and effectively teachers language to students of all languages. Available in Spanish and English with other languages coming soon.

All may be purchased through major foreign language catalogs, or you may send for current prices directly from:

Vibrante Press
P.O. Box 51853
Albuquerque, New Mexico
87181-1853
505-298-4793

Perfect Pics For Language Learning   www.vibrante.com   ©Vibrante Press